Original title:
Growth in a Clay Pot

Copyright © 2025 Creative Arts Management OÜ
All rights reserved.

Author: Rory Fitzgerald
ISBN HARDBACK: 978-1-80581-907-3
ISBN PAPERBACK: 978-1-80581-434-4
ISBN EBOOK: 978-1-80581-907-3

A Resilient Echo

In a little pot, a seed did sprout,
Wobbling around, it danced about.
A sprig so tiny, with dreams so tall,
It giggled softly, 'I might just fall!'

The sun it tickled, the rain it dripped,
A gardener chuckled as he sipped.
'What's this? A flower or a little clown?'
The roots just jiggled, not feeling down.

Layers of Existence

Inside a pot, oh what a show,
An onion sprouted, all in a row.
Each layer peeled back, a new surprise,
It told a joke, to everyone's eyes.

A radish jumped in, full of flair,
'Let's throw a party, everyone share!'
The carrot chimed in, 'I'll bring the tunes,'
While the herbs giggled, under the moons.

Little Journeys of Green

A sprout took a trip, on a sunny day,
With giddy excitement, it danced away.
'Where to next?' it wiggled with glee,
A leaf whispered back, 'Let's climb the tree!'

With petals a-flutter, they reached for the sun,
Silly adventures, oh what fun!
They stumbled, they giggled, the sky so wide,
In this little journey, they all took pride.

Roots in the Rain

A plant pranced wildly as raindrops fell,
'I love a good shower, can't you tell?'
It splashed in puddles, frolicked with cheer,
Brought the neighbors, quaking with fear!

In muddy attire, it twirled around,
With roots made of gumbo, it boogied down.
The raindrops were music, a comedic spree,
In this muddy dance, all felt so free!

Shadows of the Garden

In the garden, plants play hide and seek,
They stretch and yawn, feeling quite unique.
A carrot giggles, tickled by the sun,
While daisies whisper, 'You're number one!'

But mushrooms sulk, saying, 'It's not fair!'
They grumble in the dark, wishing for some cheer.
The radishes wear hats, so bright and proud,
Saying, 'We're the coolest in this leafy crowd!'

Cultivating Dreams

Little seeds are dreaming, deep beneath the dirt,
Plotting their adventures, while avoiding hurt.
They're wishing for a playdate, with the warm, soft rain,
While a busy worm says, 'Let me entertain!'

A sprout shimmies, claiming it's a whale,
It splashes through the mud, telling quite the tale.
But the snails just chuckle, slow with their delight,
Thinking, 'Oh, the stories from this silly fight!'

The Fight for Light

In a crowded pot, a stem began to shove,
It said, 'Excuse me, I need some room to love!'
A leaf replied with sass, 'I was here first, you know!'
They jostled for a chance to bask in the glow.

A pebble chimed in, rolling with a grin,
'Why not just share? You both can win!'
So they lifted their leaves and swayed in delight,
Finding joy together in their fierce little fight.

Budding Through Barriers

A tiny bud poked through a crack in the pot,
Saying, 'Hey world, look what I've got!'
Its petals were colorful, but slightly askew,
Proud of its journey, from the dirt it just blew.

A pebble smirked, 'You think you're so bold?'
The bud laughed back, 'I was just a seed, behold!'
With each little wobble, it danced and it spun,
Singing, 'Who needs barriers? I'm just here to have fun!'

Embracing Constraints

In a pot where dreams are small,
A cactus learns to stand up tall.
With roots that curl like twisted spaghetti,
It waves at dirt, saying, 'Don't be petty.'

The limits here feel like a hug,
While ants march by, giving a shrug.
Each inch of space is a tiny dance,
In this compact world, they take their chance.

Warmth Within Earthen Walls

In cozy clay, the ferns all laugh,
The sun shines down, a cheerful staff.
Buds peek out like giddy kids,
Hiding in pots, their secret bids.

Each raindrop feels like a ticklish tease,
Where lazy roots sway in the breeze.
With every drop, a giggle sprouts,
In this snug home, no room for doubts.

Journey of a Bud

A little bud wakes up at dawn,
Singing songs of the backyard lawn.
Its pot is small, but dreams are vast,
It stretches out, having a blast.

With every poke at the clay's embrace,
It giggles, 'Look at my brave face!'
From dirt to sky, it's quite a ride,
In this snug space, it takes on pride.

From Soil to Stardust

From muck and mud, twinkles rise,
A pot of wonder meets the skies.
Dance like dust, twist like a leaf,
Every blunder feels quite brief.

In this vessel of earthy cheer,
A wink of sunlight draws them near.
Stars in clay pots, who could foresee?
That space can hold such jubilee!

Veins of Hope

In a pot with roots below,
A plant said, 'Look at me go!'
Dancing stems and leaves so spry,
I'm aiming for the sun up high.

Sunshine brings out my best glee,
A sassy sprout, oh can't you see?
With each new leaf, I play the game,
Water me, and I'll bring you fame!

Tenacious Blossoms

Tiny buds in a cozy space,
Stretching out to find my place.
Through cracks and bends, I make my way,
A plucky bunch, ready to play.

With a smile and a cheeky wink,
I'll bloom, no matter what you think!
My petals wink at the gloomy sky,
"Ha! I'm sprightly, just watch me fly!"

Fragility Meets Strength

Oh, here I stand, a delicate sight,
But watch me shine with all my might!
When the wind blows, I might sway,
Yet I laugh, 'I'll be here all day!'

A touch so soft, like whispers of spring,
Yet deep inside, oh, the strength I bring!
With roots so firm in this cozy nest,
I giggle and bloom; I'm simply the best.

Whispered Promises of Tomorrow

In a pot that's cracked and chipped,
I dream of days when I won't be zipped.
Whispers of promise with each raindrop,
Soon I'll pop out, and I won't stop!

"Hey there, world! Ready to play?"
I call out loud, come what may.
Life's a dance, I shall embrace,
Even in clay, I'll find my place!

Roots Beneath the Surface

In a snug little pot where the good soil hides,
The roots dance like dancers on joy-filled rides.
They wriggle and giggle, having quite the fun,
Hoping to sprout like rays of the sun.

They whisper secrets to the earth below,
"Got room for a party? We love to grow!"
The neighbors are rocks and there's dirt everywhere,
But these vines are wild, they just don't care!

Silent Strength of the Soil

The soil chuckles softly, a secret so sly,
Holding dreams of green leaves as time passes by.
"I'm a pillow of hope for all roots you see,
Just waiting for buddies, come party with me!"

Worms wiggle with pride, slinking under the sun,
"Just look at our job, well isn't it fun?"
They're stylists for roots, doing hairdos so grand,
Creating an underworld rock and roll band!

Blossoms Underbound

Underneath the surface, a party's in bloom,
Petals plotting escapes from their cozy small room.
They're painted with laughter, a splash of delight,
Hoping to sneak out for a wild, wild night.

"Let's burst through this pot, we've been here too long!"
They bubble with joy, and they start to sing songs.
But the stubborn old clay just chuckles and smirks,
"Come on little blossoms, just wait till it works!"

The Hidden Struggle

It's a struggle, a tussle beneath the hard crust,
Roots jockey for space, in each other they trust.
"Who knew growing up could be such a chore?
But let's keep on digging, I refuse to be sore!"

A little sprout giggles, "Why can't we just break?
This pot is so cramped, for goodness' sake!"
Yet through the tight squeeze, they chuckle with might,
For even in struggle, they're bound for the light!

Breathing in Light

In a pot with a grin, so round and so bright,
A sprout peeks out, full of delight.
With a stretch and a yawn, it dances up high,
Reaching for sunshine, oh my, oh my!

Wiggling its leaves like a feathered fan,
It's plotting a party, oh what a plan!
With raindrops as guests and soil as cake,
This little green troublemaker's wide awake!

Chasing the shadows, it bounces around,
Making friends with a worm, oh, how they are bound!
They giggle and wiggle, what a silly crew,
In their little pot world, the fun just flew!

At dusk they unwind, and the stars start to peek,
Telling tales of the sun, now the moon's at its peak.
In the pot of laughter, where dreams take flight,
Who knew being small could feel so right!

Surrender to the Sun

A little green thing in a pot so snug,
Winks at the sunlight, gives it a hug.
With each passing ray, it twirls and spins,
Shaking off doubts like worn-out skins.

It's got a bold plan for a sun-soaked day,
To stretch and wiggle in a daring display.
"Catch me if you can," it giggles with glee,
As the sun tries to melt it, oh such a spree!

With leaves raised high like a hand in class,
It dances with shadows as moments pass.
Surrender to warmth, it sings a sweet tune,
Inviting the bees to join in the swoon.

The night brings a lull, and the world feels tight,
But not for this sprout, it'll always take flight.
Tomorrow's another day to bask and to play,
In its pot of jollity, come what may!

The Art of Resilience

In a cozy little pot where mischief can grow,
A sprightly green fellow puts on quite a show.
With a wobble and a giggle, it stands up so tall,
Proving to critters it won't ever fall.

A gust of wind brings a curious swirl,
It leans to the side, but what a brave twirl!
With roots snug underground, it takes a firm stand,
"I'm here to stay," it announces so grand.

A storm rolls in, but it's ready to play,
Dancing in raindrops, come whip, come sway.
With mud on its leaves and a grin ear to ear,
This tiny green warrior has nothing to fear!

As the sun peeks out, with a chuckle and cheer,
It lifts its small voice, "What else can I clear?"
In a world of clay pots, where laughter is spun,
The art of resilience is so much fun!

Cradled by Nature

In a clay cradle, so warm and so tight,
A plucky little sprout takes its first bite.
With dirt on its cheeks and a smile so wide,
It squeaks to the sky, "Let's go for a ride!"

The ants in a line march by with a hum,
"Hey, look at us! We're not just a crumb!"
The sprout waves its leaves, "You're all welcome here,
Let's throw a grand party, bring everyone near!"

With worms as the band and rain as the drink,
They dance in their pot without a blink.
The heartbeat of nature, it pulses with glee,
In this lively pot world, where all are so free!

At the end of the day, when stars fill the space,
It snuggles in deep, finding comfort in grace.
In its clay home, full of laughter and mirth,
Who knew little sprouts could celebrate birth?

Hold My Hand

Hand in hand, we take a dance,
In this soil, we find our chance.
Roots tickle deep, we giggle loud,
Shaking off the dirt, we're proud.

Sunshine cheeky, tickling leaves,
Waving at the clouds with ease.
We stumble, trip, then laugh a lot,
Planting dreams in our tiny pot.

In clay confines, we stretch and play,
Bouncing sprouts come out to say:
"Here we are, let's joke and tease,
Watch out, world! We're born to breeze."

Side by side, with laughter bright,
We sprout our hopes, take joyful flight.
In our little earth of bliss,
Let's hold our hands and plant a kiss.

Earth

Oh dear earth, you messy friend,
You bring us smiles that never end.
With worms and mold, you mix the fun,
Around your grounds, we laugh and run.

Digging deep, we find surprise,
Gooey hands and filthy thighs.
In clumps of dirt, we take a stand,
Crafting kingdoms with a grand plan.

Rolling slopes of grassy cheer,
We come to plant both hope and fear.
With every clod, a giggle grows,
This earthy game, everyone knows.

So here's a toast to mud and clay,
In every form, the fun we lay.
Let's revel in our quirky place,
Together in this happy space.

Rising in Soft Embrace

Like shy sprouts under morning light,
We stretch and yawn, what a delight!
Wrapped in warmth, we rise with glee,
A little poke from earth, whee!

Tickled by the raindrop's dance,
We sway around, a playful chance.
In cozy clay, our dreams expand,
Hugging the warmth with leafy hands.

With giggles soft from roots below,
We reach for sky and steal the show.
In funny poses, we extend,
Life's a joke, and we're the blend!

So let's embrace this clay parade,
Through muddy trials, we won't fade.
With every laugh that we create,
We bloom together, oh so great!

Life's Quiet Revolutions

In stillness, we begin to spin,
A leafy laugh, we're all in.
Turning circles, pots so round,
Roots take charge, yet soft and sound.

Silent whispers, secrets bare,
In each corner, it's fun to share.
The quiet moves of green and brown,
World's a theater, we get down.

With tiny leaves, we break the mold,
Stories sprout that must be told.
In gentle nudges, we will grow,
Crafting fun in every row.

Let's celebrate each little win,
As life's revolutions dance within.
In every laugh, our joy ignites,
In this stillness, dream delight!

From Darkness to Dawn

In shadows cast by great tall trees,
We bloom with giggles, catch the breeze.
From darkened pots, we twirl with glee,
A dance of laughter, just wait and see.

As dusk descends, the stars come out,
We whisper dreams, we twist and shout.
In cozy corners where we lie,
From darkness sprouts our funny high.

With morning's light, we stretch and sway,
Throwing twinkling giggles this way.
From snuggy beds of earth we rise,
Ready to conquer earthly skies.

So here's to light, the dawn we greet,
In our small world, we can't be beat.
With every laugh, the day we've won,
From shadows to the shining sun!

Within the Confines

In a tiny space, how can it be?
A sprout with dreams of a grand marquee.
Roots are dancing, feeling so fine,
Too big for the pot, but it's still divine.

A flower's voice sings, oh so sweet,
"I'm cozy here, but need more heat!"
The walls echo, 'Just wait a sec,'
As everyone laughs, what the heck?

Birds on the ledge, they sing with glee,
"We all need some room, can't you see?"
The plant just grins, arms up in cheer,
Says, "This pot's my throne, I'll conquer here!"

But when the rain comes, oh what a show,
Dancing in droplets, just letting it flow.
Bouncing like crazy, a wild career,
Who knew such joy lived right in here?

A Journey Encased

In a pot so snug, I plot my escape,
While dreaming of lands beyond the drape.
A snail rolls by, says, "Why hurry?"
"You're living the life, it's all a flurry!"

The bumblebees buzz, with tales to share,
Of flowers and fields, oh the fresh air!
I wiggle with envy, like a sock on a dog,
Trapped in my mug, like a tea-loving frog.

But wait! What's that? A tiny seedling sprouts,
It's got spunk and sass, no fears or doubts.
"Let's take on the world, just us two!"
With dreams of the sky, and morning dew.

Through the cracks of the pot, we try to see,
What lies ahead in a land that's free.
Laughter erupts as we plan our spree,
A journey encased, how grand it can be!

Nature's Grit

With grit and a grin, I poke through the dirt,
"I may be small, but I won't be curt!"
Each crack a challenge, a ticket to play,
I'll dance with the worms, hip-hip-hooray!

The breeze gives a laugh, sways me about,
"Keep pushing up, you'll never pout!"
My neighbors chuckle, the weeds all nod,
"Look at her go, this little green pod!"

A ladybug lands, all shiny and bright,
"Patience, my friend, you're a marvelous sight!"
So I stretch like I'm yawning, spreading my leaves,
"Let's conquer this pot; oh, such fun it weaves!"

Every inch gained is a riotous tale,
A race with the raindrops, let's set our sail!
With nature's grit, watch us all unfold,
In life's little pot, we're a sight to behold!

Slumbering Possibilities

In my cozy pot, I snore with delight,
While dreams of forest dance in the night.
The sun peeks in, a warm gentle nudge,
"Wake up, little friend, don't you want to budge?"

I yawn and I stretch, with a sleepy grin,
"Can't I enjoy this nap I'm in?"
The clouds above giggle, snickering near,
"Rise up, shine bright, there's nothing to fear!"

The moon whispers softly, a lullaby tune,
"Dreams blossom brighter beneath this buffoon!"
So I wiggle and wiggle, breaking the calm,
With thoughts of adventures, wrapped up in charm.

Awake from my slumber, I'm ready to roam,
Within these clay walls, I'll make it my home.
With humor and hope, the best of my frame,
Slumbering possibilities, I'm igniting the flame!

Bound by Boundaries

In a vessel snug and tight,
A little sprout sparks delight.
Its dreams are big, oh what a sight,
But it's stuck in this clay, oh what a plight!

With walls that cramp and snugly squeeze,
It wiggles and jiggles, oh, such a tease!
A tiny voice in the pot does plea,
'Let me out, I wanna make some trees!'

What's a plant to do for fun?
Plotting escapes under the sun!
"Maybe I'll poke a leaf, just one,
And hope that nature knows I've won!"

But for now, in this snug abode,
It plays hide and seek on the road.
"Just wait till I'm free, I'll explode!
You'll see! I'll be the plant you all code!"

Stretching Towards the Sky

Underneath the wide, blue dome,
A little root calls this pot home.
It dreams of a sky, wide and chrome,
With fluffy clouds where it can roam.

It stretches its leaves, reaching high,
'Touch the clouds, oh me, oh my!'
It wiggles and jiggles, oh why, oh why,
Can't it poke its head and say 'Hi'?

The neighbors, oh they snicker and cheer,
'You're still here? You're such a dear!'
The pot chuckles, what a peculiar sphere,
As the sprout rolls its eyes, shaking off fear.

With each tiny push, it breathes in fate,
Determined resolve, never late.
One day it knows it will break out of state,
To twirl with the clouds and celebrate!

Nurtured Silence

In the quiet of the pot's embrace,
A sprout practices its pokey face.
With all of its might in a funny race,
To see if this space will become more ace.

The wind whispers jokes of the open lawn,
The clay giggles back, oh what a con!
This silence is nutty, enough to yawn,
As roots salute the next day's dawn.

In a chorus of gurgles and little taps,
The tiny plant hushes the giggly chaps.
"Shush, folks, I'm bustin' out of these wraps,
With dreams of jungle and mappy mishaps!"

Pot's squishy hug is the softest dress,
Full of warmth but it feels like a mess.
Yet in this stillness, there's much to express,
A secret potential, delicately blessed.

The Dance of Sprouts

In a pot where the sunbeams twirl,
Tiny leaves begin to swirl.
With roots that jive, and branches furl,
This dance of sprouts causes hearts to whirl!

A cha-cha of green in a confined space,
Each sprout turns left, a wiggly race.
Branches high, all smiles on each face,
Making the most of this silly place.

Wait, what's that? A party under the rim?
A tiny bug joins in on a whim.
They spin and leap, oh isn't it slim?
In this pot, life's vibrant and dim!

With laughter echoing near and far,
A concert of nature, what a bizarre!
Though bound and muzzled, they find who they are,
In the dance of sprouts, they're all a star!

Hidden Potential

In a pot, a seed sits tight,
Dreaming of the skies so bright.
Wiggling roots with goofy glee,
What's the rush? It's just a tree!

Every inch feels like a mile,
Dancing dirt, it likes to smile.
'Just wait,' says the sun up high,
'You'll be a giant by and by!'

The water's splash, a silly dance,
A tiny sprout takes a chance.
'Hello, world! Can you hear me?'
This little dude is now so free!

Tiny Warriors of the Soil

In the dirt, they battle hard,
Tiny roots with tiny guard.
Waging war on weeds so mean,
Brawling bravely, like a dream!

Armed with light and drops of dew,
With little boots, they march anew.
'Fear not!' says one with leafy swag,
'We'll show them all! Let's raise a flag!'

The soil shakes with laughter loud,
As warriors face their leafy crowd.
'Take that, pesky bug!' they shout,
Tiny champions, there's no doubt!

Cultivating Dreams

In a pot, dreams intertwine,
A sprinkle here, a twist of thyme.
'Let's bake a cake of sunshine bright,
With sprigs of joy, it's outta sight!'

Mixing hopes like herbs so fine,
A scoop of laughter, no decline.
'Add a dash of rain today,
It's a recipe for play!'

Tiny leaves begin to stir,
Magic moments start to purr.
With every sip of morning air,
They twirl and leap without a care!

Tender Footsteps

Pitter-patter, roots peek out,
With hopeful dreams and lots of doubt.
Each little step a comedy,
Shaking soil, chuckling with glee!

In this tiny, jolly pot,
Footprints dance, the world's their lot.
'Where to next?' they ask with flair,
'Perhaps a leap to anywhere!'

Up and down, they twirl and play,
Every moment's a bright bouquet.
Through sun and shade, they jiggle on,
'Tender steps make us so strong!'

Barriers to Blossoms

In a pot, a plant sits shy,
Waving leaves, oh me, oh my!
Roots are tangled, feeling stuck,
"Why's the world so out of luck?"

Sunlight peeks with a bright grin,
"Hey there, pal, let's begin!"
I stretch my leaves, feeling free,
"Watch me dance, just wait and see!"

Neighbors laugh, it's quite a scene,
Plastic faces all so green.
But they can't stem my silly cheer,
"I'll be the jester, never fear!"

Finally, I'm let loose to roam,
Chasing sunbeams far from home.
Barriers, break! With a flick!
I'm the star, the plant, the trick!

Sowing Surprises

Digging deep with a little shovel,
Planting seeds can cause quite a bubble.
"What will sprout?" I gleefully yell,
"A broccoli tree or a potato shell?"

Topped with dirt, I wait in glee,
Every day, there's a mystery!
Sprouts poke out, each a surprise,
"Potato blooms or clouded skies?"

One day it rains, I do a jig,
Out pops something, I'm feeling big.
It's a weed! "Oh what a tease,"
Laughing hard, "I'll grow with ease!"

All around me, chaos reigns,
Laughter ties us with sweet chains.
Planting joy in every crack,
In this garden, there's no lack!

Breaking Free in Silence

In quiet clay, there's panic galore,
Roots whisper "let's explore!"
Trapped within, it feels so tight,
"Being still? That's not my plight!"

Poking a leaf, it brushes the brim,
"What's outside could be a whim!"
Daydreaming of breezes and light,
I giggle in my pot, pure delight.

A crack appears—this is my shot,
With a wiggle, I'll give it a trot.
Bursting forth, it's quite the feat,
"I'm free now—so let's meet!"

Silently loud, I join the air,
Puffed up with pride, daring to dare.
Look at me—such a dandy spree,
From quiet clay, I now roam free!

Invincible Dreams

In a pot, I dream with flair,
Maybe I'll grow legs, who knows where?
Floating clouds or mountains high,
Looking down from a pie in the sky!

Each little leaf feels a gentle breeze,
"Life is grand! Let's do as we please!"
Bouncing thoughts as bright as spring,
With every wiggle, I jig and sing.

I spy a bird; I'll follow it far,
Join in their fun, and raise a star.
"What's stopping me? That's just a myth,
A clay pot? Oh, that's just a rift!"

Invincible dreams make shadows quake,
With every leap, delight I make.
So here's to dancing, flying too,
In my heart, all skies are blue!

Entwined in Earth

A sprout peeks out with a curious grin,
In a cozy container where it all begins.
Dirt smudged on its face, but who can complain?
It's a jungle in here, and it's learning to feign.

Worms throw a party in this miniature space,
They groove and they wiggle, they're setting the pace.
The plant shakes its leaves to the rhythm of glee,
Who knew that the soil could turn into a spree?

Little roots dance, they're so eager to stand,
Poking and prodding, they're making their plans.
"Stick with the clay," they all giggle and cheer,
And throw a wild bash when a raindrop is near.

The sunbeams beam down, like a golden parade,
While the plant strikes a pose, unafraid and unfrayed.
Might be a small pot, but the party is grand,
In this silly romance between earth and a hand.

Mud and Miracles

In mud pies of joy, the seedlings all play,
With laughter like bubbles that pop every day.
They wiggle and jostle in their little brown throne,
Planning their life as if they're on loan.

With a wiggle and squirm, the roots spread their cheer,
As they sip on the rain, with a slurp and a leer.
"Who knew being soggy could feel like a win?
We're fabulous here, let the fun times begin!"

Pot after pot, they look eye to eye,
Making a pact, "Let's reach for the sky!"
They'd trade in their sunlight for a wild disco,
Twist like a dancer, put on quite a show.

With dirt on their cheeks and mud in their hair,
They giggle and wiggle without any care.
In a world made of clay, the humor is thick,
Where every day's magic, as they all do the trick.

Resilient Hearts

In a pot of ambitions, a dream took its flight,
A tender green heart grew with all of its might.
Dancing through fertilized nights full of dreams,
Its laughter erupts like sprightly sunbeams.

With dirt-caked schemes and plans afoot,
Each little leaf sings, "Don't let us be boot!"
They giggle and wiggle, poking out roots,
While plotting escape in their muddy new suits.

"Hey, let's make a garden just for us three,
A wild little place where we roam wild and free!"
But is it too cozy? Could we break out in style?
The vision seems high, but we'll grow for a while.

In this quirky embrace, they grow cheeky and bold,
Resilient and funny, their stories unfold.
With roots intertwined, they've formed quite the crew,
Together they flourish, into life's grand debut!

The Burgeoning Within

In a pot full of laughter, a secret unfurls,
With dirt on its nose, the plant gives it a whirl.
"Keep it down, tiny roots, we need a big stage!
They'll never expect us to leap and engage!"

As sunlight creeps in, calling out every sprout,
They giggle and dance, where the fun is about.
"Let's stretch and let loose, show our colorful flair,
Bursting through limits with joy in the air!"

A chorus of blossoms all bloom with delight,
The pots become stages where dreams take their flight.
They sing to the worms and perform for the bugs,
In this merry old dance with the warm, happy hugs.

The world springs to life through each giggle and grin,
As the plant has become what's happening within.
With laughter and glee, they invite all to see,
How funny and wild this whole journey can be!

From Earth to Air

In a pot that's far from grand,
A sprout made its master plan.
With dreams to stretch beyond the rim,
It yelled, "Hey, sky! I'm coming in!"

The neighbors, they just laughed and sighed,
"What a spunky dreamer!" they replied.
But in that dirt, a vision sparked,
Soon leaves would dance where roots once marked.

Roots Beneath the Surface

Beneath the earth, a party's thrown,
With roots like arms, oh how they've grown!
"Hold on tight!" one shouted loud,
"Let's wiggle out and cheer, be proud!"

In soil so dense, they twist and twine,
While up above, the world looks fine.
But down below, it's quite the show,
Who knew mud could be so aglow?

Whispering Seedlings

Seedlings chat with a wiggly cheer,
"Can you believe we're finally here?"
They gossip tales of sun and rain,
While trying hard to dodge a grain.

"Did you see that bird? It had no clue!"
"Right!? I'm so glad we're not its stew!"
They giggle as they stretch and bend,
With hopes to sprout, they just won't end.

Cracks of Resilience

In the pot, a crack appears,
"Don't panic folks! It's just our tears!"
The plant chuckled, "Look, I'm tough!"
"Let's embrace it! Who needs to bluff?"

With every split, they laughed a bit,
"Freedom waits, so let's not quit!"
The crack became their secret door,
To laugh and dance, and dream for more!

Shadows of Ambition

In a little pot, something's sprouting,
A cheeky sprout, it's quite a routing.
Silly leaves wave, thinking they're tall,
But they barely reach the edge of the wall.

With dreams of grandeur, they waddle and sway,
"Just wait," they giggle, "we'll rule the day!"
But every gust makes them bend and flop,
Oh, little plants, just learn when to stop!

Count the raindrops, they cheer like kids,
While the sun's heat sears like base on grids.
"Short and stout," they proudly declare,
As they dance to the tune of the garden's fair.

Yet every day, they stretch a bit more,
Chasing the clouds like a worry wart chore.
Oh, shadows of dreams, so wide and free,
In a pot, what a sight, we all can see!

Oasis in a Vessel

In a pot of clay, a party begins,
Cacti in hats, with broad grins.
Desert dreams in a little oasis,
Throwing shade on any who chase us!

"Look at us bloom!" they giggle in glee,
While the pot whispers back, "Don't flee from me!"
The soil is rich, but oh so confined,
Yet they think of the outside, quite unwound.

Tiny roots wiggle, planning their flight,
While the clay wall holds them snug and tight.
"Let's start a band!" they all start to shout,
With harmonies sweet, though one is left out.

And every now and then, they glance at the sky,
"Beyond this pot, oh my, oh my!"
But laughter bubbles up, surpasses each doubt,
In this clay-bound joy, they're never without!

Celebrating Fragile Life

With petals in party hats, full of cheer,
They twirl in the pot, no worry or fear.
"Life's a fiesta! Join the parade!"
Though they're tucked in the mix, quite unafraid!

Roots wiggling wildly, crammed and tight,
Hoping for sprinkles of sunbeam light.
"What's out there?" they ponder, with squeaks of delight,

Yet nestled in safety, they giggle all night.

In their mini world of festive design,
They toast to each raindrop, sip moonlight wine.
A cactus next door tosses a tease,
"Let's see who blooms will win the next breeze!"

With fragile dreams, oh they're quite a crew,
Shouting "We're living! How about you?"
In a pot of laughter, let's laugh 'til we ache,
Celebrating life, what a funny mistake!

Beneath a Layer of Earth

Beneath the surface, where whispers play,
Tiny roots giggle, "We'll find our way!"
With dirt as a blanket, snug and warm,
Under the ground, they plot and swarm.

"Ready for takeoff!" a sproutlet quips,
While shaking the dirt off their quirky hips.
"Raise your hand!" yells one, in muddy delight,
As they wiggle and giggle, all through the night.

They dream of the sun, oh what a fuss,
"Will we be big? Or just plant-rust?"
In their little pot, secrets they keep,
While turtles and bugs laugh without sleep.

The soil holds laughter, like hidden gold,
With tales of their dreams, forever bold.
So, wait and see, from beneath they'll rise,
A motley crew with surprise in their eyes!

Secrets of the Soil

In a pot that's snug and tight,
A sprout sings at morning light.
"Hey, I'm not just dirt and clay!"
"It's my party, hip-hip-hooray!"

Roots stretch deep, like they're on a quest,
Digging down, they need a rest.
"I'm finding treasure, can't you see?"
"Just a worm, but still, I'm free!"

Leaves are dancing, what a sight,
Shaking off their morning fight.
"Excuse me, sunshine, can you share?"
"Only if you flip your hair!"

Dirty deeds done in the roots,
A party's brewing, gossipy hoots.
"Let's invite the bugs, they're fun!"
"Only if they bring the sun!"

Tangled in Possibility

A little sprout with big dreams,
Hops around, or so it seems.
"Watch out, world, here I come fast!"
"Or maybe not, let's chill at last!"

In cramped quarters, hopes run wild,
Twisting like a naughty child.
"I'm a vine! Nein, I'm a tree!"
"Whatever, just let me be me!"

A tiny bud with thoughts galore,
Pondering what's outside the door.
"Is it green? Or filled with mud?"
"Can I leap? Or will I thud?"

Clay walls giggle in the wind,
As whispers of adventure send.
"Join me, roots, let's take a dive!"
"Just keep the snacks, we'll survive!"

Claybound Aspirations

In this pot where dreams collide,
A little sprout begins to ride.
"Buckle up for life's big trip!"
"Just watch me take a little sip!"

Snug and safe, yet eyes wide bright,
Facing fears with all its might.
"Can I reach the sky today?"
"Sure! But don't just flail away!"

Dusty leaves begin to giggle,
Shaking off the morning wiggle.
"Hey, sun, can you hug me tight?"
"Not too close! You're quite the sight!"

With a wiggle and a jig,
This sprout trots, doing a gig.
"Let's make friends with every fly!"
"All are welcome, oh my, my!"

The Will to Flourish

In a pot with dreams so grand,
A sprout decided to take a stand.
"Watch me stretch, just pass the day!"
"Whoa there buddy, don't go cray!"

With leaves a-fluttering, having fun,
Burying doubts, oh what a run!
"Can I be a tree? Just watch me go!"
"Slow down buddy, take it slow!"

Little roots are making noise,
Gathering dirt with joyful poise.
"Let's party, guys! Bring your cheer!"
"Let's celebrate the dirt right here!"

A tiny sprout dreams big and wide,
Adventuring with roots as its guide.
"Here we grow, what a silly ride!"
"Dancing, laughing, full of pride!"

Unfolding Dreams

In a pot so snug and round,
Wonders in the dirt abound.
A sprout peeks out with a wink,
Life's a party, don't you think?

It dances with the morning sun,
Just wait till it's grown and fun!
Roots are tickled, leaves are spry,
A bonanza, oh my, oh my!

When rains come down, it starts to bloom,
Yet pot's still cozy; there's no gloom.
With every inch, it claps and cheers,
Pot-bound party for years and years!

So here's to dreams that sprout and sway,
In sassy pots, they dance and play.
Not just a plant, it's a wild fest,
In the pot, it's the very best!

Tender Tendrils

A curious vine in a small pot,
It stretches far, gives all it's got.
Twisting here, nodding there,
Like a toddler in a giant chair!

It tickles bugs and steals their hats,
Oh, what fun! It prances like that!
Climbing highs just for the view,
A little naked if it only knew!

Nibbling on sunlight every day,
With a wiggle here, it gleefully sways.
The pot might be tough, but the vine's so sweet,
With funky moves, it can't be beat!

In the middle of this cozy space,
It dreams of conquest, oh, what a race!
With squiggly joy, it seeks new sights,
A comical muse in all its flights!

Resilient Petals

In a pot with lots of flair,
A flower blooms, without a care.
It winks at bees in silly spins,
"Oh, come on in, bring your friends!"

With each new petal, it takes a bow,
Sassy swirls; it's got some how!
The wind, it plays a trumpet tune,
While petals dance and softly swoon.

A garden gnome gives a cheeky grin,
As petals giggle in their skin.
They're vibrant, bright, with colors bold,
In a pot, a comedy unfolds!

So let them bask, let them shout,
Waving at skies without a doubt.
These resilient petals, wild and free,
In this small pot, they'll always be!

The Heart of a Flower

In the center of a colorful view,
A flower's heart just knows what to do.
With a flip and a flap, it flirts with air,
Trying to charm every passerby there!

Its roots are giggling beneath the ground,
"This pot is cozy, but look around!"
It stretches up, trying to shout,
"Dear world, look here! I'm all about!"

When sunbeams tickle and raindrops fall,
It sways with a grin, standing tall.
Who needs a garden when you've got flair?
In this little pot, it'll rule the square!

So cheers to the petals, bright and merry,
With each silly pose, they're far from weary.
In this catchy place, they shout with delight,
The heart of a flower that's ready to party tonight!

Sheltered Ambitions

In a tiny space, I sprout my dreams,
Reaching for sunlight, or so it seems.
The pot is tight, but hey, I grin,
Who knew that victory could start with a spin?

My roots dance funny, all twisted and free,
Little by little, I anchor with glee.
The neighbors are herbs, they gossip and tease,
But I'll wear my flowers with utmost ease!

It's a daily show, the pot's on a stage,
I'll leap over limits, let's turn the page.
Tiny yet mighty, I'm growing in style,
Just wait for the day I play it worthwhile!

The rain might splash, and the sun blares bright,
In this quirky pot, I'll dance day and night.
So here's to the life that seems a bit tight,
I'll blossom in laughter, what a delight!

Potting Harmony

In a pot so snug, I wiggle and sway,
Dreaming of gardens, a bright, sunny day.
I'm the smallest in line, but what should I care?
I can't cut my roots, but I sure can flair!

All my friends say, 'You're stuck in a trap!'
But I've got style, watch me spin and clap!
I high-five the daisies, we laugh and we sing,
The secrets we share—oh, what joy we bring!

With every new sprout, my heart does a flip,
Each leaf is a dance, an epic trip.
Oh, the critters nearby, they think I'm absurd,
But I'm just a pot plant with dreams that are stirred!

A tiny abode, yet I'm never alone,
In my little habitat, I've claimed my throne.
Wiggling, giggling, I show them the way,
That joy can be found come what may!

Flourish Amidst Constraints

I'm tucked in a pot, but I'm feeling inspired,
With all this constraint, I can't feel tired.
Roots doing yoga, they stretch and they bend,
In this little vessel, I play, I pretend!

Oh, to be wild in an open field,
Yet here I am, dancing, my fate is sealed.
But with every corner, I swirl and I twirl,
A tiny pot hero about to unfurl!

Neighbors roll eyes as I'm dancing away,
But I take my stance, in my own unique way.
Despite all the odds, I'm clever it seems,
Who knew a small pot could hold so many dreams?

So here's to the struggles, the laughs, and a cheer,
A pint-sized adventure, let's put it in gear!
I'll thrive in my limits, that's my kind of game,
Watch out, world, I'm never the same!

The Spirit of Adaptation

Crammed in my pot, I'm ready to swing,
Finding my rhythm, oh, what fun it brings!
The little space sparks some wild chitchat,
"Tight isn't bad, I'm just fancy spats!"

Look at me twist, get no hints from the sun,
With leaves made for laughter, I'm bound to have fun.
'Potted in plight?' Oh, I must disagree,
Just watch as I jiggle so joyfully!

All the world's fuss? I'll just take it in stride,
In my cozy vessel, I feel like a guide.
Each inch is a victory, a quirky embrace,
Who needs the wide world, I've found my own space!

So let the winds blow; bring on the rain,
I'll dance through it all, I'll never complain.
In the realm of the snug, I thrive with my flair,
The spirit of joy is beyond all compare!

Nurtured by Resilience

In a cozy little pot, we sprout,
With roots like spaghetti, no doubt.
We wiggle and giggle, take a chance,
Dancing in soil, our little plant dance.

A sprinkle of laughter, a dash of sun,
We grow and we stretch, this is all fun.
With every tiny leaf that unfurls,
We bloom like we're queens in a world of pearls.

Watered by jokes, not just rain,
The wind whispers secrets, driving us insane.
Up we reach for the skies so blue,
With our clay home, there's just us two.

So here's to the pot, our little stage,
Where laughter and roots craft a quirky page.
We might be small, but oh what a sight,
In our funny little corner, everything feels right.

Stems of Hope

We peek from our pot, oh what a view,
With stems like spaghetti, and leaves painted blue.
Wiggling about, we have such a spree,
Twirling with joy, just my pot and me.

Sunshine our spotlight, water our cheer,
Each day a new chance, our giggles endear.
With every sprout, we make a new friend,
In this silly little world, fun never ends.

We whisper our dreams to the lazy bees,
As they roll by, laughing at all our pleas.
Growing our way, with roots tucked so tight,
In this pot of laughter, everything's bright.

So join in the jangle, dance with glee,
For life in this clay, it's just pot-tastic, you see!
With quirky little moments, we make it our own,
In this playful adventure, we've truly grown.

Unseen Forces at Play

In our little pot, there's magic today,
With worms as our pals, we laugh and we play.
Mysteries linger, in the soil so deep,
As garden gnomes ponder, and earthworms creep.

We wiggle and giggle, feeling so spry,
While ants have a conference, oh me, oh my!
Roots tickle each other, beneath clay's façade,
Cracking jokes in whispers, oh how we applaud.

The sun plays hide and seek with our leaves,
While shadows have dramedies, it's time for reprieves.
We stretch in this pot, with wonders to share,
In the chaos of growth, there's laughter in the air.

So here's to the forces that boost our delight,
In this zany little pot, everything feels right.
With sprightly companions and humor so grand,
We thrive in this space, hand in hand.

Canvas of Clay and Life

In a pot of clay, we paint with flair,
Colors of joy, in the sun's warm glare.
Tiny brushes of green dance in delight,
As we create a canvas, vivid and bright.

With every drop of rain, we splash and we play,
Mixing up laughter, as we brighten our day.
Our roots dig deep, a masterpiece true,
In this quirky gallery, it's just me and you.

We scribble our stories in the dust of our home,
Where the tiniest stalks dream, and the wildlings roam.
Sprouting tall tales of sunshine and fun,
In our clay pot world, we're never outdone.

So here's to the artistry we find in this spot,
With humor as paint, giving life all we've got.
In this canvas of moments, both merry and sweet,
We thrive side by side, our joy is complete.

Nature's Cradle

In a cozy little pot, oh so round,
A cheeky sprout has made its ground.
With roots that wiggle and leaves that dance,
It schemes to grow, given half the chance.

The sun peeks in with a mischievous grin,
While raindrops tap like they're playing a din.
It giggles and squabbles with a nearby weed,
Claiming the throne as it plants its seed.

Wiggly worms throw a wild shindig,
As petals blush bright like a green wig.
"Hold my drink," says the sprout with a cheer,
"Let's party hard, spring is finally here!"

With each little gust, it takes to the sky,
Adventurous dreams in a pot, oh my!
Nature's a clown in this quirky show,
Watch the little sprout steal the whole photo.

Life in a Vessel

In confines snug like a tiny room,
A sprout bursts forth, defying gloom.
It stretches tall like a morning yawn,
With leaves that wave like they just won a brawn.

Chasing sunlight like it's a game,
"Catch me if you can!" it calls with no shame.
Roots twist and tangle, a rodeo ride,
Each push and pull is a comical slide.

A sprinkle of water, a dance in the rain,
"Look at me go!" it shouts with no pain.
Neighbors glance over, all rooted with glee,
"Are we competing, or is this a spree?"

In this lively vessel, all put on a show,
With laughter and joy, look how they grow!
Life's a wild party in earthen clay,
Who knew that greens could be this way?

Bound Yet Flourishing

Confined in a pot, but don't you fret,
A sprout with ambition has no regrets.
It wiggles and jives, a funky little twist,
Claiming its space; it simply can't resist.

A robust little chap with dreams so large,
Starting a revolution, it's in charge!
With every leaf, it flaunts a new trick,
Living the life in a pot, oh so slick.

Despite the limits, it's going all out,
A tap dance here, and the roots shout,
"Hey, pot world, come and take a peek,
We're thriving together, so much to seek!"

The sun's a buddy that joins in the fun,
Together they plot to make the day run.
Bound yet bombastic, a curious scene,
This sprout's got plans to outrun the green.

Echoes of Potential

In a fragrant pot where laughter blooms,
A dandelion dreamer with hopes that zooms.
Echoes dance in the breeze, oh so sweet,
"Why can't I stretch out? I'd love to compete!"

It whispers to soil about climbing so high,
"Watch me transcend, I swear I'll touch the sky!"
Leaves flop around like a joyous parade,
Each little breeze sends them into a cascade.

With a giggle of roots, it says, "Take a seat!
This little green vessel can't be beat!"
The world feels small, but adventure is grand,
"When life gives you limits, just take a stand!"

In this echo chamber of dreams anew,
A sprout shouts loudly, "Look what I can do!"
With every shimmy and shy little sway,
Who knew that joy was just a pot away?

Resilience in a Tight Space

In a pot so snug, oh what a sight,
A sprout had a plan, to reach for the light.
It pushed through the soil, with gusto and flair,
While the neighbors exclaimed, "Do you even care?"

The more they all crowded, the wilder the show,
Each leaf had its own way of saying, "Hello!"
They jostled and giggled, in their cozy retreat,
Who knew a small space could be such a feat?

With roots all entangled, they plotted their schemes,
"Let's start a parade!" someone shouted in dreams.
The pot shook with laughter, the sun grinned wide,
For who needs more room when friends fill the side?

So here's to the sprouts, in their compact domain,
In tight quarters they thrive, with joy and with strain.
Resilience is messy, or so they've decreed,
In a world that's so small, yet filled with great greed.

Seeds of Change

In the earth so warm, a seed took its vow,
"I'll sprout if it takes me, I don't care how!"
The pot seemed so full, with nary a throne,
But a tiny ambition can't be overthrown.

With a wiggle and giggle, it poked through the grime,
"Look out world!" it cheered, "I'm ready to climb!"
The neighbors, bemused, they whispered with glee,
"Who knew such small seeds could cause such a spree?"

A dance of the roots, a tango of leaves,
They chuckled and jived as they grew in their sleeves.
"Let's throw a big bash," the new sprout exclaimed,
In the shade of the pot, its wild heart untamed!

So here they all dwelled, in this ruckus of change,
Each leaf in a tizzy, all dainty and strange.
The seeds of tomorrow spread joy and great cheer,
All while laughing loudly, for they had no fear.

The Whispering Pot

In a pot made of clay, with whispers so sly,
The plants shared their secrets, their dreams could not die.

"Did you hear?" said the petal, all fluffed up with spice,
"Last week, I had visions! I'm destined for rice!"

But the herb next to them just chuckled in jest,
"Oh sure! And I'll sail on a ship, don't you jest!"
They chuckled and giggled, their laughter like rain,
As they tallied their hopes in this delightful refrain.

Each leaf had a story, each root had a wish,
While the pot sat still, dreaming of fish.
The plants played it sly, with their dreams on a roll,
They tossed out their woes, and it lightened the soul!

In the shade of the whispers, they found their own tune,
Resilience through laughter, beneath the bright moon.
Oh, the clay pot might creak, yet together they gleam,
In this stew of delight, they cooked up a dream!

Limited Horizons

In a pot so petite, with horizons so low,
The plants had their dreams, which they started to sow.
"Who's going to Paris?" a sprout would declare,
While others just giggled, "We're stuck with our fair!"

Yet every small leaf, it stretched out in glee,
"Let's throw a big party! Just us and the bee!"
Tiny two-step, they danced all around,
In limited horizons, joy could still be found.

"Who needs the wide world?" a stem chimed in bright,
"When inside our small pot, we shine like the light!"
With a twist of their leaves, they plotted a prance,
Limited horizons but endless in chance.

With humor and heart, in their cozy little space,
They spun tiny tales, simply crafting their grace.
In a world that felt cramped, they flourished with cheer,
Proving laughter expands the limits of here!

Endless Dreams

Inside the confines, dreams danced in parade,
Each plant with a vision, their plans never swayed.
"I'll be a tall oak!" whispered one with a grin,
"I'll sprout out some laughter, let the fun begin!"

With each little sprout, the pot filled anew,
A chorus of wishes, all sprightly and true.
"Let's throw a grand gala, and invite all the bees!"
While the ants all clapped hands, shouting, "More cheese, please!"

So amidst all the soil, they tap danced with cheer,
In dreams that were boundless, they persevered near.
A fabric of friendships, stitched tight in their home,
Their dreams were like kites, swooping high as they'd roam!

Through cracks of the pot, each vision took flight,
In a world that was small, they felt out of sight.
Endless dreams in a pinch, still daring to beam,
For what is the limit when hearts share a dream?

www.ingramcontent.com/pod-product-compliance
Lightning Source LLC
Chambersburg PA
CBHW070324120526
44590CB00017B/2808